ARIAS IN SILENCE

FRAIL SPLENDOR

GORDON PARKS

ARIAS IN SILENCE

A BULFINCH PRESS BOOK
LITTLE, BROWN AND COMPANY

BOSTON • NEW YORK • TORONTO • LONDON

THIS BOOK WAS PUBLISHED WITH THE GENEROUS SUPPORT
OF
TIME WARNER INC.

DESIGN
BY
NICOLAS DUCROT

First Edition

Library of Congress Cataloging-in-Publication Data
Parks, Gordon, 1912-
    Arias in silence / Gordon Parks. — 1st ed.
        p.   cm.
    "A Bulfinch Press book."
    Includes index.
    ISBN 0-8212-2120-5
    I. Title.
PS3566.A73A89   1994
811' .54 — dc20   93-47352

Bulfinch Press in an imprint and trademark of
Little, Brown and Company (Inc.)
Published simultaneously in Canada by
Little, Brown & Company (Canada) Limited
Typography by SR Linotypers, Inc., New York, NY
PRINTED IN ITALY

BOOKS BY GORDON PARKS

Flash Photography

Camera Portraits

The Learning Tree

A Choice of Weapons

A Poet and His Camera

Born Black

Whispers of Intimate Things

In Love

Moments Without Proper Names

Flavio

To Smile in Autumn

Shannon

Voices in the Mirror

Arias in Silence

In gratitude to
Toni
Johanna
and
Nicolas
for
your assistance
and
unwavering encouragement

THE SEARCHER

FOREWORD

The pictures that have most persistently confronted my camera have been those of crime, racism and poverty. I was cut through by the jagged edges of all three. Yet I remain aware of imagery that lends itself to serenity and beauty, and here my camera has searched for nature's evanescent splendors. Recording them was a matter of devout observance, a sort of metamorphosis through which I called upon things dear to me—poetry, music and the magic of watercolor. Each visited my thoughts night and day—helped to extend my vision beyond plateaus I didn't know existed. Dawn found me in pursuit of wonders imposed upon the sea, land and sun, of things spawned in valleys, on hills and mountains—a withered rose, fire flickerings, birds winging the heights, sand grown white beneath fog.

Crumpling leaves became wreaths of finery. The sun burst through with its atomic mane. A lonely swan floated over dark water. Flower petals flew like fish through the night; other foliage bunched together grew into green valleys. The moon was suddenly a saucer from which I could eat; the falling leaves, food on my table.

Strange horizons beckoned through the transparency of each season, and gratefully I listened to their silence. Paint, music and camera came together like souls touching—lifting me from earth to the sky.

These things still live quietly in my house by the river—telling me that though I thought them dead they are still alive. I hope to never awake and find them gone.

Arias in Silence *is a rummaging through my imagination—finding things blooming, things living and dying with a certain elegance. Each image expresses the need for me to accept life gracefully—without trembling at the inevitability of my departure.*

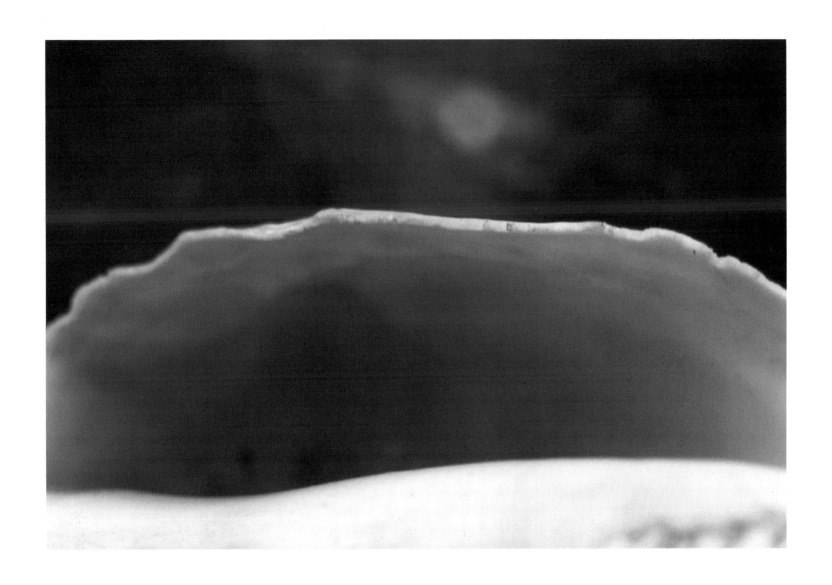

CINNABAR SKY

CONTENTS

Entries in italics refer to the poems

I LOOKED AND SAW

So many measureless things
                waiting
                waiting
                waiting—
a flower's petal,
an egg's shell,
bones from the sea,
bark of an almond tree.
So many incalculable things
to be reckoned with;
                waiting,
appeasing at long last
this weary search for serenity.

ARIAS IN SILENCE

Night had climbed the mountains.
Voices sang
from the sea, desert and woodlands.
Leaves dropped.
Stones sank deep
into earth and sand.
All such things
held to be voiceless
whispered songs of their own.
So surely I heard them
as they traveled the night.
But when to each I spoke, not one answered.
Encamped in the dream
I felt the moon touch my bed.
It smiled, lingered for a moment,
left me with a sense of something ahead.
I tried stitching those voices together,
but they hung mute in shadows.
Lately they repose in me
like a gray remembrance,
leave me with dreams so brittle to touch.
Now, when every dawn arises,
I still hear those voices singing,
even roaring at times—in silence.

UNTIL YOU ARE HERE

Spring has pushed winter aside.
No longer are new moons
scoured with cold.
Summer birds wing the horizon.
Lotus blossoms smile.
I lie here
wrapped in waiting.

Why have you not come
to lend yourself to the splendor
covering these lowlands?
I will not be left
with one untormented moment
until you are here
to acknowledge the lines
your absence paints into my brow.

THE SHELL

This soulless thing
so like stone unmoving,
awash in windblown sand,
constantly sings to me.
Its voice echoes
with the softness of blossoms
against these green mountains.
Until night drops it lingers,
then with the tide,
returns to sea
to gather in more solace.

North from the shore
is a road I take each evening.
Moonlight falls across my path
filled with whispers
my friend, the shell,
brings from the sea.
At this moment
somewhere across the distance,
it plumbs the depths   listening.
At dawn it will return
to empty me of loneliness.

THE LEAF

Assaulted by time
and relentless wind,
shorn of green and dew,
it wrinkled and fell—
A beautiful ruin crying out to be remembered.

Unable to bid it farewell
I bathed in its dust,
paying homage to graceful aging.
When my autumn arrives
I will remain captive
in the peaceful drift of its presence.

Until then I joyfully search
shores in spring wind
for the scent of blossoms
verging toward seasons
where fallen leaves gather
to make a quilt.

WATCHING A MEMORY

So often, and for years,
he had seen it up there
where sunlight paints rainbows,
where moonlight shimmers
through clouds blanketed with mist.
One sinking day he glanced up
to see it gliding downward,
magnificently wrinkled,
its green reduced to rust.
Sunlight heightened its glare.
Its shadow, drifting low, turned eastward.
On it came through a broken sky—
this very special leaf he once plucked
from his father's apple orchard.
It stopped for a moment,
observed the white in his hair
then passed on.
He returned home a little younger
to feed the splintering years
with more patience.

BRANCHES WILL FIND IT HARD TO SING

The moon,
quivering its shadow
across the river,
searches the night for blossoms
that lie in velvet mud
left over from a storm just passed.
Nature's brief need of them
was cut even shorter—
by wind that left branches bare and bruised.
For them happiness vanished
when the first peal of thunder
began arguing with the silence
falling upon this old village.

Their grief, lying now amongst brambles,
will stay
until another spring decides to begin.
Then with no blossoms left,
branches will find it hard to sing.
                Meanwhile
the moon sends its shadows on
to sift the night for reason.

FALLEN PETALS

Their color has taken refuge
in the throes of autumn.
Dawn's fingers can't reawaken them.
They lie vanquished, golden
under a jade carpet of dew.
Weak shadows spread
beneath what is left,
a hint of mortality,
as their scars darken
in this billowing dusk.

They no longer resist unlearned winds.
Even the moon grew weary
from such fierce blowing.
And here where light thins,
the blackest mountains
blackened even more.
These valiant petals
had hoped to rise,
to bloom once again.
But by nightfall
death had seized them.

THE WISH

The boy
went to sit beneath the tree
that stood thin and gnarled.
"What am I to become, Mr. Tree?"
"Whatever you wish."

The years had grown rusty
when the boy returned—a man.
The tree,
watching him stroke his beard, smiled.
"What have you become?"
"Nothing I wished to be."
"What did you wish for yourself?"
"Wisdom."
"Why did you not achieve it?"
"A lack of common sense and good reason."

Again the tree smiled.
"Wisdom is not common sense,
nor is it reason.
It is a bit of one;
a bit of the other—
with a dash of egotism tossed in."
"I lacked strength?"
The tree swayed
to a spring breeze.
"No, you lacked will.
Go back. Try again."

The mountainside fell silent.
And, with doubt in its eye,
the tree watched
the old man slowly descend
toward the lowlands.

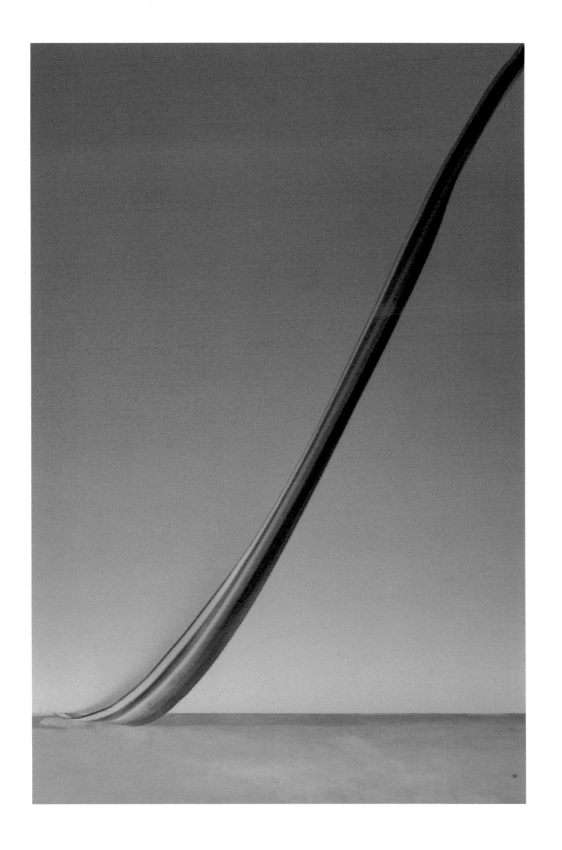

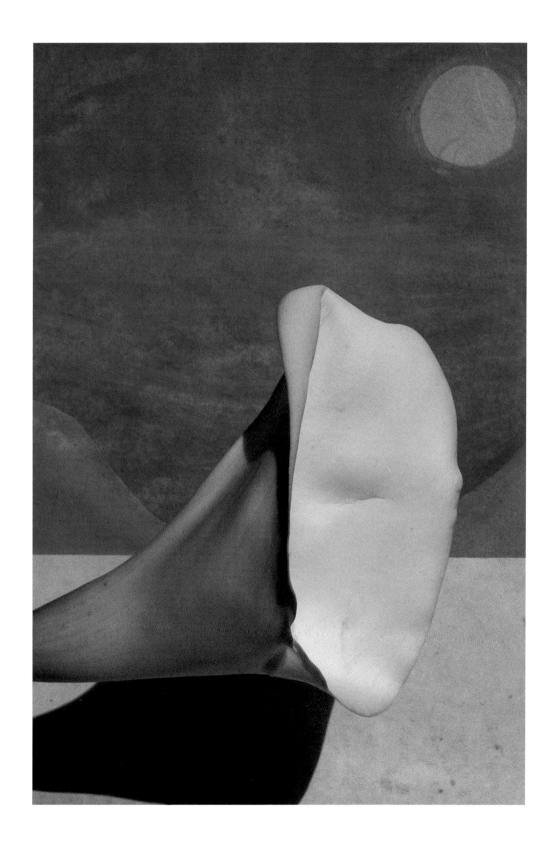

A CALLA LILY'S LAMENT

I came to bud in the shadows
of this deep gorge
from where fog soared downward
to melt a path for the sun.
Stones knew me.
Grass blades befriended me.
Rain squalls washed my blossoms clean.
Fragrant, wet with dew,
I was stirring dawn's air
when they came, tore me from my roots,
spirited me to this distant place.
Now I sit where no birds sing,
where sun hides under city smoke.
Best now that I forsake sorrow.

Perhaps in the love of some house
I will come to rest beside a window
to dream once again of my roots
spreading over asphalt heat
toward sunlit meadows.
But debauchery seems to be everywhere.
Into some house I will likely be sold
where grief will be my lot.
For the moment I sit here anguished
on a shelf of dust.

From a river long since defiled,
a cup of water came to slake my thirst.
Now, after two days' worth of despair,
I can only fasten upon memories
of my very first spring,
knowing well that spawning a lily
was not the only good it was intended for.

A GRANDSON'S QUESTION

How perfect the moon
above this eastern river.
Beneath it
      four smokestacks
      and two gas tanks
pierce the ozone haze.
My pear tree?
Can I be at peace
with brick and metal
so destructively shaped?
The question impels me
toward bewilderment.

THE MOON IS LOOKING THE OTHER WAY
(A Grandfather's Answer)

Even beneath desolate soil
roots grow with good intentions.
Step by step,
the foliage they yield
takes on fearsome shapes.
Sorcerer rain,
dark, souring and acerbic,
falls upon the green earth.
Acid has become the bitter fruit,
and the devil's delight is served.
Virtues, assigned to blossoming things,
have been set adrift
to tremble alone in the wind.
In valleys once pure,
on prairies once verdant,
in man, tree, flower, beast, sea and sky—
in everything once complete and sheened
arises the need
to stomach hostile clay.
The wind, also flawed,
spreads wrath over the woodlands.

The moon looks the other way.

TWO TRAVELING WEST

Beneath limitless stars
where waves wandered shorelines
lay a leaf.
Carried there by storm and time,
blended with rose and green,
warm in the sun's last burst,
it awaited the final trip west.
It held no need for regrets.
Its existence, though brief, had borne splendor.
Autumnal dew was now strung on it like pearls.
When suddenly its shadow darkened the sand
sadness shivered me, baffled me.
Only with the deepening night
did it all come clear.
Not for this leaf was I mourning
but for its fellow traveler
        me
through time growing thin.

THAT'S THE WAY THINGS GO

Here among sunken thistleweed
only this lone tree stands.
Wind, screaming angry,
left it with emptiness.
From the north
cold comes to harden lakes
and benumb trails with snow.
Even lordly mountains shiver.
The sky turns to ice;
and clouds, torn by its edges,
bleed as they drift.
Birds complain.
Geese cut the silence
over rivers twisting south.
Groundhogs burrow in,
frostbitten branches refuse to sway.
Frozen leaves blanket roadsides.
Summer puts its joys in storage.

That's the way things go
when winter invades.

PRAIRIE FLOWER

Abloom,
all fragrance.
Mingled with stars and moon,
its petals, even in death,
escape the carnage of autumn.
Thrice-sized, it swells and stretches—
even after seasons gather to debate.
The knife frost yields
is not to be eluded.
But the stalk stays on to drink
the dew of memory.
Bleached by autumn
it lingers in praise
from all others
dying within its sight.

NEIGHBORS

Spring has left my old plum tree
abloom in jeweled stars,
free of winter's ruthless wings,
with its shadow planted deep
into the happiness of summer.
But that young apple tree there,
leaning a bit south of the other
and burgeoning with fragrance,
unmindfully poked one branch
over that hostile wall—
where its presence is unwelcome.
My neighbor's rancor will, no doubt,
put pruning shears to it,
then pain will howl

through the innocence
of that young tree's soul.
No one would like more than I
for this blunder of youth to gather
two borderers—in joy,
to smother our differences
with blossoms soon to drop,
and miraculously align us,
lip by lip, fist by fist,
against the devil's wicked hook.

But his voice, like mine,
remains deaf to any words
that don't speak
a dozen remorseful answers.
There will be no shaking of hands.
All that time has taught us
will be of no use to the fragrance
clipped off that young apple tree.

HANDFUL OF DREAMS

I've always longed for
the promiscuity of reckless wind.
The memory that knows me best
often rolls backward to my childhood;
to my father's stallion
galloping me through wetness,
its mane flying in drenched light.
With the trees wildly bending,
across the prairie we would go
until at last only a handful of dreams
stood between us and the sea.
Hoofbeat after hoofbeat
and a pocketful of imagination
wafted us from one horizon to another.
Since those boundless mornings
not much has changed.
I am still content
to drown myself in rain
that glistens wind's reckless flights.

A FLOWER'S PLEA

Unlike most others
who don't take the time,
lean forward, reach out
and, after a fathomed look,
inhale the sweet wildness of my petals.
Filled with love
from earth, sun and moon,
I welcome your lips.
Come, take the first step.
Gaze through that indifference
separating me from those who,
after making short use of me,
toss what remains into trash cans.
Move closer. Caress me.
Kiss my blossoms.
They wear colors
torn from the secrets of gods.
Step back and see me
as I long to be seen—a joy
to live as long as time endures.

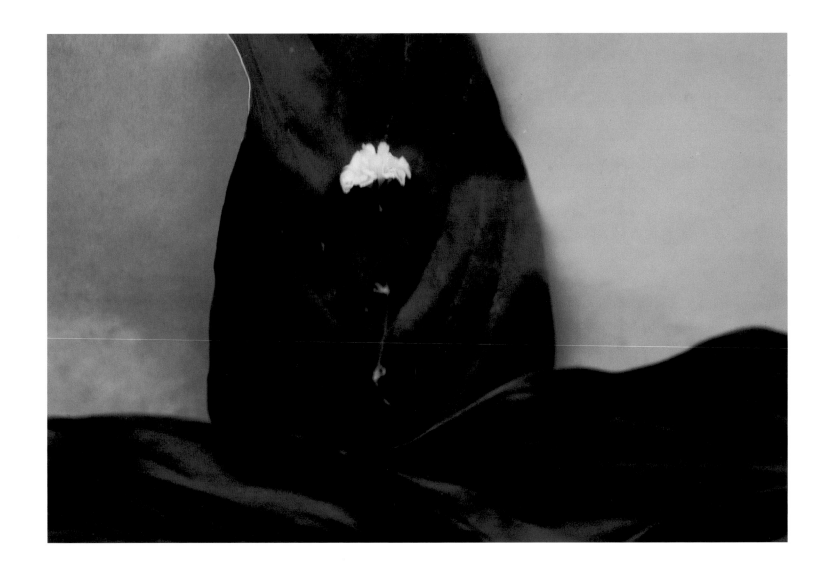

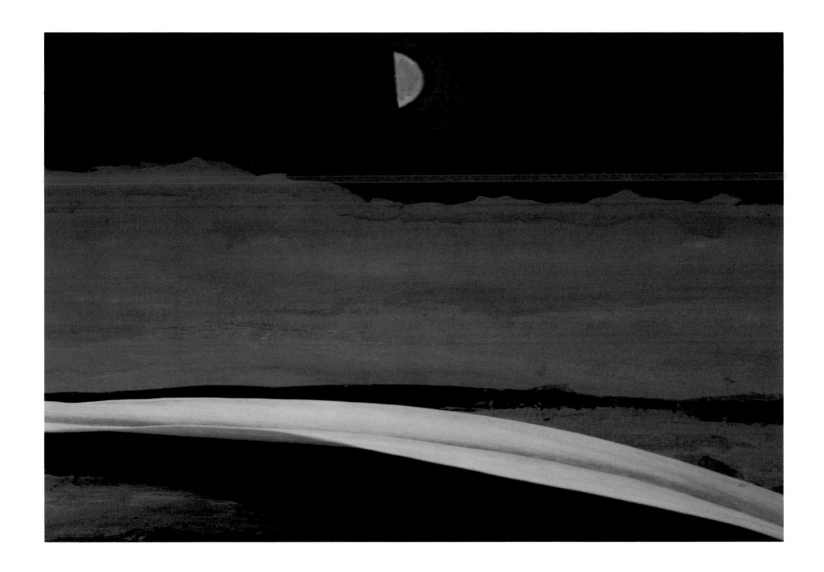

UNWELCOME VISITOR

Snow,
deceptive and unannounced,
showered like white soot
on this lazy island.
In unreadiness we neighbors of the sea
looked to the sun to calm the shiver.
The wind's treachery was predictable.
Arriving ahead of time,
it tore off leaves, scrambled them,
fed their bones to hungry waves.
Trees stand coatless.
Flowers hide between crevice and stone,
waiting until snow departs.
Stuck here we watch the sea rise toward us—
cold, uncaring, murderous.
In time spring will sneak back,
              halfheartedly,
to make friends with our impatience.
But now wind howls inside these slippery shadows.
Winter, with its frostbitten ways,
lies here contented in its icy nest.

SOUTH OF TAIPEI

One walking day south of Taipei
I came upon this river
God had laced together.
Ascending from its watersides
is a sanctuary
where yellow cranes come to roost
under alms of crescent moons.
Here, along the fringe of heaven,
virtue blends it with earth
to nurture the green of reeds;
to purge lilies of thirst.
A path of weeping willows
swaying against the moon
leads to a brushwood gate
opening to a meadow where
plum trees gorge themselves
with the sweetness of twilight.

Night had grown boundless,
the earth unearthly quiet
when I lay down to ease my aching.
The docile river meandered on
without weariness into the thickening woods,
jostling moonbeams, flickering stars.
Soon after my eyes closed
I became a lone wanderer
without sense of time lost;
without hours suffered
that amount to even a trifle.

Dawn kissed the cliffs;
dew was leaving the grass
when I awoke to a murmur.
The river—still arriving,
laden with the whiteness of fog,
embroidered with blossoms.
My heart went begging—
to forever keep me
where the patience of that river
could flow through me each morning
to leave peace.

A BRIEF DEPARTURE

Despite this avowal of regret
for my withered buds,
for each blossom gone,
I treasure the frail splendors
that gave grounds for my existence.
I was allowed my small place—
in fog, wind, rain,
gorges, mountains and meadows.
I bathed in nectar of spring
under the noontide sun.
I held no love for storms.
While enduring their frenzy
I longed for the songs of orioles;
longed to feel my roots standing hard.
With summer traveling
in some distant place,
it is bitter cold.
Mountain peaks throw shadows eastward
and winter raises havoc.
Goodbye for now.
I am off to rest.
During the joy of spring
I will come again
to overflow your paths.

I WILL BE ALL LIGHT

Summer is done with me—
the leaf, the petal, the flower.
But all is not over.
My spirit grows boundless,
soaring without worry, without tiring
through the most wreckful storms.
I see through death and refuse it.
Having known the firmness
of branches and vines;
of so many suns and moons;
of every ennobling cloud flake,
I have learned to endure.
No lament for this season.
Peace shares the space where harsh winds cry.
Summer has fallen silent,
but its virtues gather in waves.
No winter tears. No parting sorrow.
I am meant to grace this world
that blessed me with such abundance.
When this disgruntled season passes
I will wing my way back to you.
You will recognize my fragrance
strewn along your footways.
I will be all light.

GIFT

God lent us that astonishing month.
It arrived at morningtide scrubbed clean
with seaweed, jasmine and dreams.
It pervaded our rooms
with night voices
of flesh against flesh.
I remember everything,
fishbones, coral and driftwood,
bluegreen evenings of soft rain
and candle burning,
even your elaborate ceremony
of peeling oranges.

It was a time untouched
by unsmiling things.
Then suddenly it was gone,
dropped beyond the sea
like a broken star.
God lent us that astonishing month.
It's hard to believe we left it behind
to land in a garbage heap
with potato peelings
and steak bones.

DEATH CLAIMS A ROSE

Despite the lateness of spring
it had bloomed early—
while owls slept out winter
perched on the patience of a limb,
while egrets dozed above inlets
not yet touched by sunlight,
and cranes yawned
beside swollen streams.
Even while the moon drifted
through endless dark—
the rose bloomed on.
A trillion suns or more,
after brooding over its fate,
held its existence to be fleeting.
Experience had left it prudent
to habits of the seasons.
So in valleys or on prairies
where beauty is nourished,
urgency never went pleading.
Before bees came, or robins sang,
its splendid blossoms cast splendid shadows
upon April's hungry earth.
Not until October did it crumble
into such exquisite grief.

THE DISTANT HORIZON

For twelve bleeding years,
through waves of silence,
it had stared at him.
Abandoned to futility,
he had stared back while
loneliness kept dreaming in—
over the indifferent field
where beneath a stone
his woman lies;
where from eastward and beyond,
glory or hell beckoned,
offering infernal delights.

Songless birds winged the sky
toward and away from that horizon,
soaring, it seemed,
without any purpose.
He kept to himself,
missing nothing he thought,
watching moons acclaim night;

damning the pitiless sun
for ravaging so many indefensible days.
The clock moved on,
gobbling up years.
Months shrank. Time grew small.
Hours had puckered into seconds
when, with vengeance,
winter sank its teeth
into the ragged edges
of one stubborn morning.
Then impatience turned up
on his wrinkled calendar.
He looked at it closely.
A question mark stood beside it—
                    frowning.
One final swig of coffee.
He got up, sighed a long sigh
then put on his Sunday suit.
By half-past seven
he was astride his roan stallion—
galloping hard toward the city.
Dust and time would have to wait.
That unfriendly bedroom mirror
would also have to wait
before frowning at him again.

A DREAM

Angry burned the sun.
Rivers of fire raged across skies.
Clouds churned into blackness.
Heat strangled the air.
Thickly, ashes plummeted down,
blanketing seas, mountains and meadows.
My cry was soundless—
just a far-off moan in smoke,
      so soft,
it failed to contradict the silence.

Fire licking my throat
should have aroused me.
Yet hours passed, it seemed,

before I awoke and fled this dead place,
running as if hurrying from time;
wondering dazedly if I was even me.
I glanced back.
I was still there—
in ashes, smoldering.
Where fire had been
only cinders were left.

A savaging dream still hanging
like a net over a time long past.
During the burnt-out hours it returns,
like an unasked guest,
to sit darkly in a corner,
smiling in the shadow of my presence.
Perhaps it amounts to nothing,
but in these wintering years
I am inclined to wonder.

FLIGHT FROM DREARINESS

To have whatever I want;
to be free of any complaint—
both have their dangers.
Unburdened by the hard run
of everydayness,
hours, months—even years,
are rubbed out
without reason or purpose.
Complacency moves in, takes over.
I become dry as dust, bored
like a chicken, like a cow.
      Recently,
my need for passiveness
has fallen into discredit.

Give me the grinding, twisting,
topsy-turvy of any given day.
Allow the wind of uncertainty
to shake my inner branches;
to thwart the yawns
when they sag with lethargy.
This wanting besieges my heart
with the break of every dawn.

128 • DUSK LADEN